My *Five Year* Publishing Schedule

PIPER BRADLEY

ISBN: 1546541314
ISBN-13: **978-1546541318**

CONTENTS

1 YEARLY PLANS 20___

January	February	March
April	May	June
July	August	September
October	November	December

2 ACTUAL PRODUCTION 20____

January	February	March
April	May	June
July	August	September
October	November	December

3 DAILY SCHEDULE SPRING 20___
(Turn to landscape orientation)

TIME										

MONDAY	TUESDAY	WEDNESDAY	THURSDAY	FRIDAY

4 DAILY SCHEDULE SUMMER 20___

TIME											

MONDAY	TUESDAY	WEDNESDAY	THURSDAY	FRIDAY

5 DAILY SCHEDULE FALL 20___

TIME											

MONDAY	TUESDAY	WEDNESDAY	THURSDAY	FRIDAY

6 YEAR IN REVIEW 20___

Total words Written: _____

Total Books Published _____

Total Books SOLD _____

INCOME : _____

BOOKS PUBLISHED:

_____
_____
_____
_____
_____
_____
_____
_____
_____
_____
_____
_____
_____
_____
_____

NOTES

January	February	March
April	May	June
July	August	September
October	November	December

8 ACTUAL PRODUCTION 20___

January	February	March
April	May	June
July	August	September
October	November	December

9 DAILY SCHEDULE SPRING 20___

TIME											

MONDAY	TUESDAY	WEDNESDAY	THURSDAY	FRIDAY

10 DAILY SCHEDULE SUMMER 20___

TIME											

MONDAY	TUESDAY	WEDNESDAY	THURSDAY	FRIDAY

11 DAILY SCHEDULE FALL 20___

TIME											

MONDAY	TUESDAY	WEDNESDAY	THURSDAY	FRIDAY

12 YEAR IN REVIEW 20____

Total words Written: _____

Total Books Published _____

Total Books SOLD _____

INCOME : _____

BOOKS PUBLISHED:

_____
_____
_____
_____
_____
_____
_____
_____
_____
_____
_____
_____
_____
_____
_____

NOTES

13 YEARLY PLANS 20___

January	February	March
April	May	June
July	August	September
October	November	December

14 ACTUAL PRODUCTION 20___

January	February	March
April	May	June
July	August	September
October	November	December

15 DAILY SCHEDULE SPRING 20____

TIME											

MONDAY	TUESDAY	WEDNESDAY	THURSDAY	FRIDAY

16 DAILY SUMMER SCHEDULE 20___

TIME											

MONDAY	TUESDAY	WEDNESDAY	THURSDAY	FRIDAY

17 DAILY FALL SCHEDULE 20___

TIME											

MONDAY	TUESDAY	WEDNESDAY	THURSDAY	FRIDAY

18 YEAR IN REVIEW 20____

Total words Written: _____

Total Books Published _____

Total Books SOLD _____

INCOME : _____

BOOKS PUBLISHED:

_____

_____

_____

_____

_____

_____

_____

_____

_____

_____

_____

_____

_____

_____

NOTES

19 YEARLY PLANS 20___

January	February	March
April	May	June
July	August	September
October	November	December

55

20 ACTUAL PLANS 20____

January	February	March
April	May	June
July	August	September
October	November	December

21 DAILY SCHEDULE SRING 20___

TIME											

MONDAY	TUESDAY	WEDNESDAY	THURSDAY	FRIDAY

22 DAILY SCHEDULE SUMMER 20___

TIME											

MONDAY	TUESDAY	WEDNESDAY	THURSDAY	FRIDAY

23 DAILY SCHEDULE FALL 20____

TIME											

MONDAY	TUESDAY	WEDNESDAY	THURSDAY	FRIDAY

24 YEAR IN REVIEW 20____

Total words Written: _____

Total Books Published _____

Total Books SOLD _____

INCOME : _____

BOOKS PUBLISHED:

_____
_____
_____
_____
_____
_____
_____
_____
_____
_____
_____
_____
_____
_____
_____

NOTES

25 YEARLY PLANS 20____

January	February	March
April	May	June
July	August	September
October	November	December

26 ACTUAL PLANS 20____

January	February	March
April	May	June
July	August	September
October	November	December

27 DAILY SCHEDULE SRING 2021

TIME											

MONDAY	TUESDAY	WEDNESDAY	THURSDAY	FRIDAY

28 DAILY SCHEDULE SUMMER 20___

TIME											

MONDAY	TUESDAY	WEDNESDAY	THURSDAY	FRIDAY

29 DAILY SCHEDULE FALL 20___

TIME											

MONDAY	TUESDAY	WEDNESDAY	THURSDAY	FRIDAY
TIME				

30 YEAR IN REVIEW 20____

Total words Written: _____

Total Books Published _____

Total Books SOLD _____

INCOME : _____

BOOKS PUBLISHED:

_____
_____
_____
_____
_____
_____
_____
_____
_____
_____
_____
_____
_____
_____
_____

NOTES

ABOUT THE AUTHOR

Piper writes genre fiction under another pen name. The non fiction books she writes are Piper's Personal Cheat Sheets and she is happy to share those with other authors.

If you would like to receive an email when the next book will be available, OR if you have a suggestion, email her at piperbradley35@gmail.com.

Piper is not using a mailing list because lately they have been notoriously unreliable.

OTHER BOOKS BY THIS AUTHOR

Descriptive Words for Writers: *People*

Descriptive Words for Writers: *Places*

The Self Publisher's Business Notebook (available in different colors)

My Five Year Publishing Schedule (available in different colors)